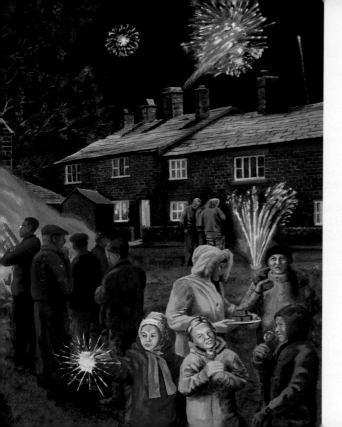

DAYS
Recipes

*Food for seasonal events
and village gatherings
compiled by
Astrid Bartlett*

*with illustrations by
Trevor Mitchell*

SALMON

THE VILLAGE YEAR

Astrid Bartlett has lived in the same Somerset village for over forty years and is one of several long-standing members on the Village Hall and Green Committee. The village calendar is marked by regular events throughout the year. Since the demise of the shop, the hall has become the beating heart of village life. As a rural, farming community, food and drink naturally play a crucial part in all these celebratory gatherings. The most popular events are repeated, while others only happen once every few years. This book contains recipes used on some of these occasions.

The Wassail

The wassail is the first of our annual village celebrations. It starts with the ritual beneath a selected apple tree on the village green. A wassail queen is chosen; toast is soaked in cider and hung in the tree while cider is poured around its roots. Shots are fired into its branches. The crowd makes as much noise as possible with pots and pans or anything else to hand in order to ward off evil spirits and encourage the tree to be fruitful. A wassail song is sung. Here is one version:

> Apple Tree, Apple Tree
> We're come to wassail thee
> To bloom and to bear
> Hatfuls and capfuls
> And three-cornered sackfuls
> And a little heap under the stairs.

After that everyone heads across the lane – festively lit with a string of colourful lights – to the village hall, where plain cider and hot spiced mulled cider is served, also apple juice and any apple-related food.

St. Valentine's Day

It is a few years since we held a St. Valentine's Day event in the village hall. Perhaps it is time for a repeat? Hearts were naturally the theme for the evening, so the hall was decked out appropriately with great big red paper hearts and Cupid's bows and arrows.

Shrove Tuesday

To mark the beginning of Lent, a pancake evening is held. Cooks come armed with their favourite frying pans – usually black and well-proved – but always hygienic. Stacks of pancakes soon appear and are as individual as the cooks.

Mothering Sunday

The half-way point to Easter, celebrated on the third Sunday in Lent, when families visit the Mother Church. Children hand out flowers picked the day before and made into pretty posies, adorned with colourful ribbons and lace. They are taken to the altar in wicker baskets, before being distributed to the expectant congregation. After the service everyone troops around to the village hall where the simnel cake is cut and served with fruit juice or sherry.

Harvest Home

This is the highlight of the village calendar, held in a marquee on the village green. Competitors arrive early in the day with their various entries, many of which are humorous. Categories vary from food to photographs, floral arrangements to limericks. In the afternoon, teams compete for a highly sought-after sporting trophy. A supper of various cold meats with mixed salads and hot buttered potatoes is followed by an impressive selection of trifles and fruit pies. Trophies are presented after the meal. A traditional barn dance, still under canvas, rounds off the evening. Coloured lights strung up earlier in the day, light the way across the lane to the village hall. For several years running, the lane was closed to traffic, allowing the fiddlers, callers and dancers to 'strip the willow' and 'dosey-doe' beneath the myriad stars and coloured lights along the narrow 'High Street'. Magical.

Harvest Festival

Not to be confused with the Harvest Home. After a thanksgiving service, lunch is served in the village hall, followed by an auction of pumpkins, eggs, apples and other harvest produce brought around from the church. There is always a wonderful selection of food on offer: colourful soups, potted meats, fish patés, local cheeses and other home-made delights, including bread rolls and a specially made harvest loaf in the shape of a sheaf of corn.

Hallowe'en
In the past it has usually been combined with a bingo session. Some villagers arrived in fancy dress, complete with broomsticks, pointy hats and black floaty outfits, adorned with moons and stars. Flickering pumpkins lit the way to the hall.

Silent Auction of Promises and Goods
We have held several of these in recent years and they are always popular. Those who have no tangible goods to offer, may promise to sell their time to dig a garden, paint a house, mow a lawn, babysit or even draw up a will. Before the cut-off time for final bids, food is served. Usually this is something simple but tasty: baked potatoes with various fillings, such as chilli con carne, vegetable lasagne or garlicky prawns.

Curry and Quiz Night
This is popular with all generations. Teams are made up from complete families, others join with friends; sometimes complete strangers get together to form a team. It is a good way to get to know a new neighbour in a convivial atmosphere. Food is served at the half-way point.

Apple Day
This is celebrated in October and as the title implies, is exclusively apple-related. There are various stalls on the village green. One would have bottles of different coloured apple juices. On another, people try their hand at producing the longest unbroken apple-peel from a Victorian-style apple peeler. Yet another has a miniature cider press for villagers to make their own juice from a nearby tub full of apples.

Royal and National Celebrations
Generally speaking, we are a patriotic village and enjoy upholding age-old traditions. In recent years we have had both the Queen's Diamond Jubilee and the Royal Wedding to celebrate. For the wedding we held a barbecue on the green. The Jubilee celebrations involved an upmarket afternoon tea in the hall, complete with a splendid iced cake representing the union Jack. Flags were flown from cottages, houses and farms all around the village. Festive bunting was draped outside the hall and around the green.

Messy Church

This is the latest innovation in the village hall, for children to meet together in a fun atmosphere. Dedicated volunteers gave up their time in order for the children to enjoy a new experience. On the first occasion they decorated an altar cloth, especially for harvest and made a prayer tree as well. They then got stuck into food preparation, on this occasion pizzas – which they later all enjoyed together. That was followed by apple crumble. The second event included sausages and rolls and the making of lanterns to carry around to the church, just in time for the annual carol service.

Christmas Gathering

This is held on a Saturday night, as near to Christmas as possible, trying to avoid any clashes with local carol services. The gathering is a chance for the Hall and Green Committee to thank the villagers for their support throughout the year. Spiced mulled wine is served along with hot sausage rolls and mince pies. Carols are sung accompanied by an accordion, guitar or piano. Christmas-themed poems, readings or monologues are recited. There is an activity trestle for the youngsters, where imaginative table decorations are magicked out of a selection of berries, leaves, candles and tinsel. The evening ends with a final few carols and Christmas songs for all to join in, before heading home, usually beneath a wintry, starlit sky.

New Year's Eve Celebrations (or Bonfire Night!)

Instead of Bonfire Night on November 5th, our village celebrates New Year's Eve with a huge bonfire and spectacular fireworks. Wedges of parkin, flapjacks and other delights are on offer, along with hot sausage rolls. These are washed down with spiced mulled cider, poured from steaming jugs for the adults and warm fruit juice for the youngsters.

Work Party Fodder

Once or twice a year, work needs to be done in the hall such as tidying-up store cupboards or chucking out items no longer needed from under the stage. There is also the village green to keep tidy: trimming trees, or filling holes in the car park. Manual labour is hard work, so we all welcome the food and drink break, washing the food down with mugs of hot tea or coffee.

Index

Cover pictures *front:* Summer Fête *back:* Funfair on the Green
title page: Bonfire Night

Printed and published by J. Salmon Ltd., Sevenoaks, England © Copyright

Spiced Mulled Cider

*After being chilled with cold or soaked by rain on the village green, there is nothing
more welcoming than the smell of hot, spicy mulled cider. The last time we celebrated
the wassail, the aroma of the evening lingered in the village hall for days afterwards
and was still apparent when the Parish Council met the following week.*

**4 pints cider   A stick of cinnamon   A few cloves
Some grated nutmeg   A few allspice corns
2 washed and quartered apples (unpeeled and uncored)
A washed and quartered, unpeeled orange
A piece of peeled root ginger, cut or bruised to release its full flavour
About 4 to 6 oz. demerara sugar or honey to taste
A little brandy for extra kick**

Pour the cider into a large saucepan. Add the various spices, the quartered apples,
orange and cut or bruised ginger. Add the sugar (or honey) and stir until the sugar has
dissolved or the honey has melted. When really hot but not boiling, add the brandy.
Taste to adjust the flavour; you may want to add a little apple juice or water.

Quick Fix Cheese Sandwich with Apple Chutney

Enduring the wet or cold on a freezing winter's evening, can make one really hungry. Coming indoors to the sanctuary of a warm village hall smelling of spiced cider, feels like sheer heaven. This open sandwich fits the bill perfectly in terms of food satisfaction.

**A small baguette   Some slices of your favourite local cheese
A smearing of British butter   A decent dollop of apple chutney**

FOR THE APPLE CHUTNEY:
**2 lb. apples (after peeling and coring)   1 lb. finely chopped onions
½ pint vinegar   12 oz. sugar   1 tsp. pickling spices
4 oz. mixed dried fruit   1 tsp. salt   A generous teaspoon ground ginger
A small piece of dried chilli for a bit of extra warmth and bite**

Put the finely chopped onions into a saucepan with a small amount of the vinegar. Simmer until soft. Add chopped apples, ginger, salt, mixed dried fruit and spices, including the chilli (tied in muslin). Add a tiny bit more vinegar to prevent contents sticking to the pan. Simmer until the fruit is soft. Stir occasionally. Add the rest of the vinegar. Stir in the sugar until it is dissolved. Boil until chutney thickens. Remove the muslin bag of spices. Pour into hot jars and seal.

An alternative to chutney would be slices of raw eating apple, cored and with the peel left intact – but this may be more suited to a summer's day than in the deep mid-winter.

Victoria Sandwich Hearts

You will need two heart-shaped baking tins for this recipe. The baking tins may vary in size. If your tins are small, you could make two cakes from this amount - but then you may run the risk of accusations of being a 'two-timer'.

6 oz. self-raising flour   3 eggs   6 oz. butter
1½ tsp. baking powder
6 oz. sugar   Grated zest of an orange
Raspberries for topping and raspberry jam for the filling

Put the flour, butter, zest and sugar into a bowl with the eggs and baking powder. Beat well until consistently creamy throughout. Butter the heart-shaped baking tins. Using a pair of tins for each complete cake, divide the mixture evenly between the baking-tins. The length of cooking time will depend on the size of your cake. Cook until golden and springy to the touch. If making only one big cake, expect it to take about 25 minutes at about gas mark 4 or 180°C (350°F) and proportionately less time for the smaller ones. When cooked and cooled, sandwich together with raspberry or strawberry jam. Top with fresh raspberries/strawberries in the shape of a heart or two overlapping hearts.

Strawberry Hearts

Although these are classed as biscuits, they are more of a cross between a biscuit and a scone. The last time I made these, I divided the mixture into two, adding some currants, lemon zest and ground ginger to the second half and baking them for the same length of time as the original mixture.

4 oz. sugar
4 oz. butter
4 oz. soured cream or natural yoghurt
12 oz. plain flour
1 beaten egg
1 tsp. baking powder
Strawberry jam

Beat the sugar and butter together. Add the beaten egg. Mix in the soured cream/yoghurt. Add flour and baking powder. Beat well. Roll out dough on a floured surface. Using a heart-shaped biscuit cutter, cut out the biscuits. Make a small depression in the centre of each heart. Fill the depression with strawberry jam. Bake at about gas mark 4 or 180°C (350°F) for about 12 minutes until golden. Leave to cool on a rack.

Trevor Mitchell

The Basic Pancake Mixture

To mark the beginning of Lent, a pancake evening is held. Cooks come armed with their favourite frying pans – usually black and well-proved – but always hygienic. Stacks of pancakes soon appear and are as individual as the cooks. Fillings may include lemon juice, sugar, jams, berries and cream. Savoury cheese pancakes are cooked to order with a choice of chopped chives, apple slices, diced ham, mushrooms or similar. Until the pan is properly proved, the first pancake usually breaks up (chef's perks). Using a small pan is preferable to a larger one for this recipe.

4 oz. plain flour   ¼ tsp. salt   1 egg   ½ pint of milk   lemon juice

Place the flour in a bowl and add the salt. Make a well in the centre and crack the egg over the bowl. Gradually beat the egg into the flour with a small quantity of milk. Beat well until the batter is smooth, adding the rest of the milk gradually. Once you have a good thick, even batter, allow it to rest for about half an hour. Pour contents into a jug to make it easier to regulate the amount used. Heat the pan. When pan is hot, add a little oil. Pour a small amount of batter into the pan and swirl it around to cover the entire base. Flip pancake over when golden and cook the second side. Slide onto a warmed plate. Squeeze over some fresh lemon juice and a sprinkling of sugar or use any of the above suggestions for an alternative filling. If making a savoury pancake, cook the first side then flip the pancake over. Mentally divide the pancake into three sections then fill along the central strip. Flip one side up over the centre to cover the filling. Then flip the second side over to make a tidy tubular, open-ended parcel. When the cheese melts and dribbles out, the pancake is ready.

Simnel Cake

The half-way point to Easter, celebrated on the third Sunday in Lent, when families visit the Mother Church. Flowers picked the day before are taken to the altar in wicker baskets, before being distributed to the expectant congregation. After the service everyone troops around to the village hall where the simnel cake is cut and served with fruit juice or sherry.

1 lb. almond paste   Apricot jam   Egg white

FOR THE CAKE:
6 oz. muscovado sugar   6 oz. butter   3 eggs   6 oz. self-raising flour   6 oz. sultanas
6 oz. currants   1 oz. candied peel   grated lemon zest   1 tsp. mixed spice

Divide the almond paste into three equal pieces. Roll out and cut two circles using the loose-bottomed cake-tin base as a template. Cream sugar and butter together in a bowl and add the eggs Carefully stir in all the other ingredients (apart from the jam, egg white and reserved almond paste). Blend well. Put half cake-mix into the buttered cake-tin lined with baking parchment. Smooth the mix. Place one of the almond paste circles on top of the cake mixture. Add the remaining cake mix. Smooth the top. Cook at gas mark 2 or 150°C (300°F), for 2¼ hours. Cool cake. Heat the apricot jam a little to enable it to spread more easily. Cover the top of the cake with the apricot jam. Place the remaining almond circle on top. From the final piece of almond paste, make 11 balls. Place the balls at even distances around the top of the cake using the egg white as glue. Brush the top of the cake with the remaining egg white. Place under a hot grill for a couple of minutes until golden.

Basic Scone Mix

This is a most enjoyable way to spend a summer afternoon with pleasantly challenging tasks to fulfil. All are catered for: the very young, the elderly, the active and wheelchair-bound. Clues are left hidden around the village in little boxes. For the children, there are pictures to collect, such as different bugs and insects. Adults have anagrams to unscramble and cryptic clues to solve. At the village hall a sumptuous tea is served and small prizes given to the winners.

8 oz. self-raising flour   2 oz. butter   ½ tsp. salt   ¼ pint milk

Put the flour into a bowl with the salt. Add the butter – cut into small pieces; rub it into the flour until evenly blended. Make a well in the centre and add the milk. Draw the mixture together until you have a soft ball of dough. Place the dough onto a floured surface and roll out to the thickness of about ½ in. Cut into rounds with a pastry cutter – using whatever size you prefer. Place on a buttered baking tray and cook for about 10 minutes at gas mark 7 or 220°C (425°F). Cool on a wire rack. To serve, cut horizontally and spread with clotted cream and raspberry jam or butter and strawberry jam or whatever else takes your fancy.

For savoury scones, add any of these to the dry mixture, before adding the milk:

**1 tsp. baking powder   4 oz. finely grated Cheddar cheese   ½ tsp. dry mustard
Some black pepper   Teaspoon paprika   Chopped chives   Finely grated onion
Chopped fresh sage   Small chunks of diced apple**

Chocolate Brownies

Most people love any chocolate-related recipe. The addition of cranberries, dried fruit, chopped dates or diced apple will not only make this mixture go further but taste delicious too. The addition of chocolate chips may be regarded as a step too far - even for chocoholics.

3 eggs   8 oz. soft, dark muscovado sugar
6 oz. self-raising flour   2 oz. cocoa
A handful of cranberries
4 oz. sunflower/rapeseed oil or softened butter

Whisk the eggs and sugar until creamy and well blended. Add the oil or butter. Whisk in. Sieve the flour and cocoa together and stir carefully into the egg and sugar mix. (If you whisk at this point the dry ingredients will go everywhere.) Once the powdery ingredients have been well incorporated you can then use a whisk. Add the cranberries or fruits of your choice. Stir well until fully blended. Tip the mixture into a 9 in. square baking tin. Dot the top with a handful of cranberries or quartered glacé cherries. Bake for about 25 minutes at gas mark 4 or 180°C (350°F). Cool for a short while in the tin and then cut into 16 pieces.

Trevor Mitchell

Trifle

Sponge fingers are traditionally used for the base of this recipe but a better alternative, if you have the time, is a home-made Victoria sponge sandwich; it soaks up the sherry perfectly.

One layer of Victoria sponge sandwich   Sherry
Raspberry jam   One banana, thinly sliced
Custard   Double cream
Fresh raspberries or other soft fruit such as loganberries
Egg white   Grated zest of a lemon   A little icing sugar
Fresh soft fruits for the topping

Make your Victoria sponge (4 oz. self-raising flour, 2 eggs, 4 oz. butter, 4 oz. sugar, orange zest). Place the cooled sponge in the base of a fruit bowl or serving dish. Pour over enough sherry to cover the top of the sponge and be absorbed by it. Spread jam over the top of the sherry-soaked sponge. Place the soft fruit berries of your choice over this. Thinly slice the banana and scatter it on top of the berries. Make the custard. Allow it to cool. When cool, spread it over the fruit. Whisk the cream. Whisk egg white in a separate bowl. Add the two together. Add grated zest of one lemon and add this to the egg white and cream mix. Sprinkle in a little powdered icing sugar to taste. Stir carefully. Spread this sweetened lemony cream over the top of the trifle and decorate with fresh fruit or grated chocolate.

Fruit Pie

The first apples of the season are used to make this recipe. In a bad year – or when the crop has been delayed – apples frozen from a previous year are used and taste almost as good. A mixture of cooking apples and eating apples is perfect for a fruit pie as the cooking apple falls when cooked but the eating apple adds a little crunch and texture to the finished product.

8 oz. shortcrust or rough puff pastry
1 lb. cooking apples   ½ lb. eating apples
A little water   Sugar to taste

Optional: **cloves / cinnamon / lemon zest / handful of raisins / blackberries / loganberries**

First peel and core the apples. Cook gently in a saucepan with a little water. Add any of the above optional additions. Once the cooking apples have fallen, put aside to cool. Add sugar to taste. Divide pastry into two, one piece a little larger than the other. Roll out into two circles. Line a buttered pie dish with the larger piece of pastry. Fill the pastry with the cooled, cooked apple. If using cloves, remove them at this stage. Place the rest of the pastry on top, sealing with water and crimping the edges. Trim. Roll out the leftover pieces and cut into shapes: leaves, hearts, stars, animals, etc. Place these attractively on top and secure with a little water. Make a hole in the centre of the pie for the steam to escape. Cook until pastry is golden (about 20–30 minutes) at gas mark 4 or 180°C (350°F).

Broccoli and Blue Cheese Soup

This is a really pretty speckled soup, reminiscent of the colours of spring. It's tasty too.

12 oz. broccoli
1 oz. butter
A large onion, chopped
1 leek, chopped
1 potato, chunked
1 pint chicken stock
½ pint milk
4 oz. crumbled blue cheese such as Stilton
Black pepper
Salt

Wash the broccoli and break into florets, reserving a couple of small ones for the garnish. Melt the butter in a large saucepan. Cook the onion and leek until soft. Add the stock, broccoli and chunked potato. Simmer together, with a lid on the saucepan, for about 20 minutes. Cool a bit before pouring into a blender or liquidiser. Add the milk and adjust the seasoning. Reheat in the saucepan and add the crumbled blue cheese. Allow the cheese to melt but not boil.

Potted Meats

*Some wonderful flavoursome spreads or faux patés can be made out of leftover cooked meat.
As well as appearing at the harvest festival lunch, they are also handy for picnics or a
quick snack and are delicious on toast. You can play around with different meats,
herbs and spices to achieve this. Below is a good basic recipe for leftover cold, lean beef.*

POTTED BEEF

About ¾ lb.-1 lb. finely minced leftover cooked beef   2-3 oz. butter
Herbs such as dried marjoram or basil to taste   A little salt and freshly ground black pepper
A pinch of paprika and/or ground coriander

Melt the butter in a saucepan. Add the minced beef, herbs, spices and seasoning. Stir
well until evenly blended. Press into small pots and seal with a layer of melted butter.

POTTED GAME

Using the same method as above, strip the cooked meat off the carcass of whatever
game you are using: pheasant, rabbit, pigeon, etc. Mince it finely. Use in the ratio of
3:1 meat to butter.

Meat from any game of your choice   Minced onion   Crushed garlic   Allspice   2-3 oz. butter
Black pepper   Dried herbs of your choice   Natural sea salt

Melt the butter in a saucepan. Add the cooked minced meat. Add whatever herbs and
spices you fancy: minced onion, crushed garlic, allspice, dried herbs, salt and pepper.
Test for flavour and adjust accordingly. Put into jars or pots and seal well with
clarified butter.

Trevor Mitchell

Smoked Salmon Terrine

This looks particularly attractive, especially once it has been sliced as the pinky-orange layers are reminiscent of seams of coloured strata running through white rock, almost like a Neapolitan ice cream.

9 oz. smoked salmon
8 oz. cream cheese
2 tbsp. dill or parsley – or a mixture of both
Black pepper
2 tbsp. horseradish sauce
4 oz. softened butter

Divide the salmon into four. Butter a 1 lb. loaf tin. Line the tin with cling film, leaving a good overlap all around. Cover the inside base with strips of salmon and a twist of black pepper. Put the cream cheese, butter and horseradish into a blender with the herbs of your choice. Place a third of the resulting mixture onto the smoked salmon base. Layer until you finish with final strips of salmon. Pull up the sides of the cling film as tightly as you can. Press firmly on top. Put in the fridge for a minimum of 6 hours. When chilled, carve into slices. Garnish with a sprig of dill or parsley. Serve with a salad and wedges of lemon.

Blood-Red Pepper Soup

It is a while since we held one of these evenings. In the past it has usually been combined with a bingo session. Villagers arrive in fancy dress, complete with broomsticks, pointy hats and black floaty outfits, adorned with moons and stars. Flickering pumpkins light the way to the hall. Bingo night is one of the rare occasions when we are lazy about cooking and usually buy-in fish and chips. However, a fine alternative would be a good hot warming, blood-coloured soup, served with yoghurt 'cobwebs' and scary crusty rolls.

A tsp. olive oil   A crushed clove of garlic
4 red peppers, de-seeded and chopped   A large chopped onion
A small sliced de-seeded, fresh red chilli pepper
3 tbsp. tomato purée
1½ pints chicken stock   Zest and juice of a lime
Thin strips of pared lime rind   Salt and black pepper

Heat the onion and peppers gently in the oil for about 5 minutes until softened. Add the crushed garlic, sliced chilli, tomato purée and about half the stock. Simmer for about 10 minutes. Cool slightly. Purée in a liquidiser. Add remaining stock, lime juice, zest and salt and pepper. Bring to the boil. Decorate with yoghurt cobwebs or garnish with thin strips of lime rind. Serve with scary crusty rolls.

Scary Sun-dried Tomato Bread Rolls

If you are enjoying some blood-red pepper soup, you really have to team it up with some form of bread. What better accompaniment than these scary sun-dried tomato rolls?

1 lb. strong white bread flour   1½ tsp. salt
2 tsp. sugar   1 oz. butter
2 oz. finely chopped sundried tomatoes
2 tbsp. sundried tomato paste
½ tsp. easy blend dried yeast
9 fl.oz. lukewarm milk
Reserve a few chopped tomatoes for 'teeth'

Put all the dry ingredients into a bowl. Rub in the butter. Add the chopped tomatoes and the tomato paste. Mix together with your fingers. Add the yeast. Finally add the milk. Knead on a lightly floured surface. Shape into a ball. Leave to rise in a buttered bowl in a warm, draught-free place until doubled in size. Take out and re-knead into rolls. Press a few chopped tomato 'teeth' into one side, in the shape of a scary grin Place on a buttered baking sheet and allow to rise again. Cook at gas mark 5 or 190°C (375°F) for about 20 minutes until they are golden and hollow-sounding when tapped underneath.

Garlicky Prawns

If you are using fresh prawns, shell them. Put shells in a pan. Cover with cold water.
Bring to the boil. Discard the shells but retain the liquor to flavour the sauce.
A mixture of king prawns and small prawns makes an interesting combination

If possible, a mixture of fresh king prawns and small prawns – but frozen ones will do
2 oz. British butter
2 oz. flour
A little root ginger
1 clove crushed garlic
A little ground coriander
A little fresh red chilli pepper
Milk

Melt the butter in a pan and add a small piece of the chopped red chilli pepper. Add a small piece of peeled root ginger and ground coriander. Add the crushed garlic. Stir. Add the prawns and cook until they absorb the flavours – about three or four minutes. Remove the prawns, chilli and ginger. Discard the ginger and chilli. Keep the prawns in a warm dish. Add the flour to the flavoured butter and mix until it forms a roux. Add the milk a little at a time, stirring with a balloon whisk to prevent lumps. If you have the liquor from the shells, use it now. When the sauce is just right, return the prawns to the pan and stir well.

Quick and Easy Vegetarian Curry

*Surprisingly, for those who love their meaty curries, they may
well find they do not even notice there is no meat in this dish.*

**A little butter/oil or a mixture of the two
An onion, roughly diced   Crushed clove of garlic
An apple, peeled and roughly diced   Sweet pepper (any colour)
A stem of leek, trimmed, washed and finely sliced**

A mixture of whatever vegetables you have to hand which may include:
**Butternut squash, peeled and diced   A handful of raisins
Carrot, peeled and diced   A handful of currants
Swede, peeled and diced   A handful of sultanas
Potato, peeled and diced   Flesh and juice of an orange or tangerine
Your favourite curry paste – or make your own from pounding and mixing spices together
Salt and pepper**

Heat the butter/oil in a large pan. Add the onion, garlic, diced apple, chopped pepper
and leek. Cook until soft but not brown. Add the curry paste or ground spices. Stir
well. Add the rest of the vegetables, fruit of your choice and the dried fruit. Stir well
to coat with the curry spices. Add enough water to cover. Stir again. Bring to the boil
and simmer until tender. Taste and adjust seasoning if necessary. Thicken with a little
cornflour if needed. Serve with fragrant basmati rice, raita, naan breads and pickles.

Naan Breads

It is great fun making your own naan breads. You can decide what size and what flavours to add, or you could just have plain ones. Here is a basic recipe with some suggestions for additions.

1 lb. plain flour	¼ pint warmed milk
½ tsp. salt	2 tbsp. vegetable oil
1 tsp. baking powder	5 fl.oz. plain yoghurt
2 tsp. sugar	1 egg, lightly beaten
2 tsp. dried yeast	

Suggestions for added flavour – to be added after mixing all the dry ingredients together from first column and before moving on to the second column: the 'wet' column:

Ground coriander   Dried basil   Dried marjoram   Crushed garlic   Black pepper

Put all the dry ingredients into a large bowl. Add any or all of the suggested ingredients for added flavour. Add the wet ingredients. Mix well. Knead for about 10 minutes. Place in a lightly oiled bowl. Allow to rise in a warm place for about an hour. Once doubled in size, re-knead into tear-drop shaped naans, whatever size you prefer. Cook on a hot cast-iron plank, or on a griddle or hot plate of an Aga for about 3 minutes each side. Turn over and cook the other side for a further 2–3 minutes.

Apple Soup

1 lb. cooking apples
½ pint white wine
1 pint water
Sugar to taste

Chop the apples but do not peel or core.   Simmer the apples in a pint of water in a large saucepan, until tender.   Rub through a sieve.   Add the wine.   Stir in the sugar while still warm.   Chill.   Ladle into soup dishes and garnish with lemon rings.

For an alternative: add the zest and juice from two oranges or add a teaspoon of mixed spice/cinnamon or a couple of cloves, at the apple-simmering stage.

Crab Apple Jelly

Apples are so versatile and vary from the tiniest little red crab apple to the massive great dumpling-sized Bramley cooking apple. There are several apple orchards in the village, mainly for cider but also for cooking and eating (and occasionally for scrumping). The crab apple is perfect for making a clear, topaz-coloured jelly which looks so attractive in its jar. It tastes delicious and is an ideal accompaniment to complement all sorts of meat and game, especially roast lamb and venison.

Gather your fruit – say 4 lb. crab apples. Decide what flavour you would like: ginger, lemon, clove, maybe all three or just as it is. Wash and cut up the apples but don't peel or core. Put in a saucepan with the flavourings. Add just enough water to cover the apples. You will need about 2–3 pints of water to cover 4 lb. of crab apples. Simmer for about an hour until the fruit is soft. Strain the juice through a sterilised (or scalded) jelly bag. Be patient and allow the juice to drip through naturally without being tempted to give the jelly bag a squeeze. This way you will have a perfectly clear finished product. Measure the juice. For every pint of juice, use 1 lb. of sugar. Place the juice back in a clean pan. Add the sugar and stir until dissolved. Bring to the boil. Boil rapidly until set (setting point is 220°F). Pour carefully into sterile jars and seal.

Marinades for Barbecues on the Village Green

The oil in the marinade helps the star of the barbecue to stay moist; the acidity with the addition of wine, citrus juice or vinegar, aids in the tenderising process. Monkfish is a good, meaty fish to barbecue, as is salmon. Fresh mackerel and sardines are another delight as they are good and oily and do not usually stick to the enveloping foil. Place the fish on a bed of the herbs of your choice on a rectangle of foil, maybe with a slice of lemon on top and a twist of black pepper, then parcel them up.

FISH MARINADE:
Crushed garlic   Ground rosemary/dill
Olive oil   Balsamic vinegar
Ground coriander   Salt
Black pepper

You do not really need any depth to the marinade as long as all sides of the fish have been covered.

Place the fish into a shallow dish with the marinade. Turn the fish over at least once making sure all sides have been in contact with the mixture. Twenty minutes will probably be long enough to infuse flavour and do all the necessary magic with your fish.

Meat needs a little longer in a marinade than fish to reap the full benefits.

BEEF OR VENISON MARINADE:
Balsamic vinegar   Olive oil
Torn basil leaves/dried basil   Ground coriander
Salt   Freshly ground black pepper   Crushed garlic

Treat the meat in exactly the same way as you would the fish. Place the chunks in a shallow dish and make sure the marinade has touched all its surfaces. If necessary, turn it over several times to achieve this.

FRUIT AND VEGETABLE MARINADE:
Olive oil   White wine vinegar
Salt and pepper   Crushed garlic
Mixed dried herbs/chopped parsley

Put all the fruit and vegetables into a large bowl and mix thoroughly with your hands to ensure the marinade has covered everything. Thread fruit and vegetables onto kebab skewers. If you wish you can intersperse the fruit and vegetables with chunks of meat before putting on the barbecue.

Garlic Bread

What better accompaniment can you have to a barbecue than garlic bread?
This is simple to make and truly delicious.

A French stick
Crushed garlic
Butter or a mixture of butter and olive oil spread
Salt
Chopped parsley or mixed dried herbs
A little black pepper (optional)

Put the butter/butter mixture into a dish. Mash it until soft with a fork. Add the crushed garlic, salt, herbs and pepper. Mix until all the ingredients are evenly distributed. Lie the bread down on a breadboard and cut in half. (This just makes it easier to handle.) Stand each of the cut halves on end, cut-side down. Slice lengthways down the two upstanding halves. You now have four equal-sized pieces. Butter the four pieces with your herby, butter-garlic mixture. Either place on a baking sheet and cook in a hot oven for about 4–5 minutes. Or wrap up in foil and place on the barbecue until heated through. Once cooked, cut or break into chunks to accompany the other barbecue foods.

Child's Play Quick and Easy Pizza

8 oz. mix of scone dough
A can of tinned chopped tomatoes, drained of juice
Crushed garlic   Ground black pepper
Grated Cheddar cheese or mozzarella
Basil/oregano/snipped chives

A choice of options: **mushrooms, salami, ham/bacon, red, green or yellow peppers, anchovies**

FOR THE SCONE DOUGH BASE:
8 oz. self raising flour   2 oz. British butter
¼ pint whole milk   Pinch of salt

Measure the flour into a bowl. Add the butter and salt. Finger the butter into the flour until it is similar to breadcrumbs. Add the milk to form a soft dough. Knead gently. Roll out on a lightly floured work surface and place on a buttered pizza tin base. Stir the crushed garlic evenly into the drained and chopped tomatoes. Spread this mixture over the entire dough base. Add the toppings of your choice from the list above. Finally, top with the cheese and herbs of your choice. Cook until the cheese is soft and the pizza dough cooked thoroughly.

Trevor Mitchell

THE ROYAL OAK

Spiced Mulled Wine

What better start can you have to an evening than the welcome whiff
of spiced mulled wine as you enter the hall?

THIS MAKES ABOUT A LITRE:
A bottle of red wine   7 fl.oz. water
4 tbsp. dark brown sugar   Allspice   Some grated nutmeg   Thinly pared orange peel
A cinnamon stick broken in two   A chunk of peeled root ginger
A quartered whole orange   Half a dozen cloves

Optional: **A small nip of brandy for extra kick – added at the last minute**

Put all the ingredients into a large pan – a preserving pan is ideal. Heat through gently to just below boiling point. Stir until the sugar has dissolved and the spices have flavoured the entire concoction. Turn down the heat. Add the brandy at this point, if you are using it. Jug it out to serve in warmed glasses.

If mixing your own spices, to prevent bits of unwanted spices getting into the serving glass, muslin bags can be bought from most ironmongers. Or you can make your own from a square of muslin, tying the top with a loop of thin string, making it easy to remove when necessary.

If you are unsure of spice quantities, you can always use ready-packaged mulled wine spice sachets, easily available at whole food outlets and delicatessens.

Mincemeat

Any Christmas gathering would not be the same without mince pies. Here is a simple recipe for making the mincemeat to fill them. If you mix it a couple of weeks in advance, the flavours will be fully melded together. The only cooking involved in this recipe, is the apple. The rest is just a case of chopping, grating and mixing.

½ oz. butter   1 lb. finely chopped apples
8 oz. currants   8 oz. raisins
8 oz. sultanas   4 oz. candied peel
4 oz. chopped dates   8 oz. soft, dark muscovado sugar
6 oz. suet   Juice of 1 lemon
Grated lemon rind   1 tsp. cinnamon
1 tsp. mixed spice   ½ tsp. grated nutmeg
4 tbsp. brandy

Melt the butter in a pan. Add the finely chopped apples. Cook gently until the apple has softened. Remove from heat and allow to cool completely in a large bowl. Once cold, add all the other ingredients. Mix well. Store covered, in a cool dark place, stirring occasionally over the next 24 hours before potting into sterile jars.

Sausage Stuffing Rolls

*Almost everyone loves a hot sausage roll – and what better than a special
Christmas-flavoured one, made with pork sausage meat and herbs?*

1 lb. pork sausage meat
A finely grated onion
A finely grated apple
1-2 tbsp. breadcrumbs
A small bunch of freshly chopped sage leaves (or a teaspoon mixed herbs, dried or fresh)
Salt and black pepper

Put the sausage meat into a bowl. Add all the other ingredients. Squish the mixture between your fingers to get them all evenly distributed. Mould into small sausage shapes. Cook for about 10 minutes. Remove from oven. Allow to cool. Once cool, wrap in puff pastry and cook as you would a normal sausage roll.

Don't be frightened of working with different herbs and spices. Some wonderful flavours have been discovered by the serendipity of experimentation.

Flapjacks

1 tbsp. golden syrup
4 oz. demerara sugar
6 oz. British butter
4 oz. sultanas
A handful of chopped dates
About 8 glacé cherries, halved
1 heaped tsp. ground ginger
A little orange or lemon zest
8 oz. porridge oats

Soak the sultanas in boiling water to allow them to swell. Melt butter gently with sugar and syrup in a saucepan. Add ginger and zest. Drain the sultanas and add them to the saucepan with the dates and glacé cherries. When the butter has melted, remove saucepan from heat source. Add the oats and stir well. Spoon into a 9 in. square baking tin. Cook for about 20 minutes or until cooked and golden. Allow to cool slightly before cutting into slices, squares, wedges or fingers.

Trevor Mitchell

Parkin

*This is always popular and usually the first food offering
to disappear as soon as it is placed on a plate.*

**9 oz. plain flour   7 oz. sugar
4 oz. porridge oats   2 heaped tsp. ground ginger
5 oz. British butter   7 oz. golden syrup
3 oz. black treacle
A rounded teaspoon bicarbonate of soda
1 dsp. vinegar   ¼ pint milk**

Put the flour, sugar, oats and ginger into a large bowl. Melt the butter in a pan over a gentle heat. Add the syrup and treacle to this mix. Once melted, pour the melted mixture into the dry ingredients in the large bowl. Add the bicarbonate of soda and the vinegar to the centre of the mixture. It should fizz. Put the milk into the syrup saucepan and heat slightly. Swish it around to gather up any trace of treacly syrup. Add to the mixture and stir well. The mixture should now resemble batter. Pour into a roasting tin which has previously been buttered and floured. Bake for about an hour or so in the middle of the oven – at about gas 4 or 180°C (350°F). Allow to cool before cutting into squares. This is one recipe which improves with keeping as long as others allow you to.

Shortbread

4 oz. plain flour
2 oz. ground rice
4 oz. butter
2 oz. sugar

Mix the flour with the rice. Add the butter. Rub it in. Stir in the sugar. Knead lightly until it forms a smoothish dough. Butter a 7 in. round baking tray. Place the dough onto a lightly floured work surface. Roll it out in the shape of the baking tray. Carefully lift it into the baking tray. Crimp the edges with your fingers and thumb. Prick all over the surface with a fork. Score the top into 8 wedges which will break easily once cooked. Chill until it is good and firm before baking. Place in the oven at gas mark 3 or 170°C (325°F) for about 35 minutes. Cook until a pale golden colour. Allow to cool for a few minutes before removing carefully onto a wire cake rack.

Date and Walnut Cake

The pairing of some ingredients is similar to marriages made in heaven. Basil and tomato spring to mind, also egg and bacon and cheese and pickle. Another perfect pair: date and walnut.

3 oz. British butter
8 oz. dates
¼ pint boiling water
3 oz. sugar
1 egg
8 oz. self-raising flour
1 tsp. baking powder
3 oz. roughly chopped walnuts

Put the chopped dates into a bowl and cover with the boiling water. While the dates are steeping, you can proceed with the next step. In a large bowl place the butter, sugar, egg, flour and baking powder. Beat until properly blended. Add the walnuts. Add the dates along with the liquid they are in. Stir well. Spoon well into a well-buttered 2 lb. loaf tin. Bake in an oven gas mark 4 or 180°C (350°F) for about 1¼ – 1½ hours. Check that the cake is well-risen and firm before removing from the oven. Allow to cool in the tin before removing carefully and placing on a wire rack to cool.

Speckled Bread (Bara Brith)

There are umpteen versions of this recipe; I seem to have tried and tested most of them.
Here is just one simple version, not using yeast.

10 oz. self-raising flour
1 beaten egg
½ pt. of strong tea
8 oz. soft, light brown muscovado sugar
12 oz. mixed, dried fruit

Place the sugar and dried fruit in a bowl with the hot tea. Stir and leave the fruit to swell for as long as you are able. If you are using tea-bags, remove them at this point. When ready, stir the flour and egg into the mixture. Line a 2 lb. buttered loaf tin with cooking parchment. Mix thoroughly before turning the mixture out into the loaf tin. Smooth the surface of the cake as much as possible. Bake in an oven gas mark 2 or 150°C (300°F) for about 1¾ hours until firm and well-risen. Allow to cool in the loaf tin for about 10 minutes before placing carefully on a wire rack to cool thoroughly. A little butter spread on the cooled, finished product may be a trifle indulgent, but it is delicious.

Trevor Mitchell

METRIC CONVERSIONS

The weights, measures and oven temperatures used in the preceding recipes can be easily converted to their metric equivalents. The conversions listed below are only approximate, having been rounded up or down as may be appropriate.

Weights

Avoirdupois	Metric
1 oz.	just under 30 grams
4 oz. (¼ lb.)	app. 115 grams
8 oz. (½ lb.)	app. 230 grams
1 lb.	454 grams

Liquid Measures

Imperial	Metric
1 tablespoon (liquid only)	20 millilitres
1 fl. oz.	app. 30 millilitres
1 gill (¼ pt.)	app. 145 millilitres
½ pt.	app. 285 millilitres
1 pt.	app. 570 millilitres
1 qt.	app. 1.140 litres

Oven Temperatures

	°Fahrenheit	Gas Mark	°Celsius
Slow	300	2	150
	325	3	170
Moderate	350	4	180
	375	5	190
	400	6	200
Hot	425	7	220
	450	8	230
	475	9	240

Flour as specified in these recipes refers to plain flour unless otherwise described.